Paulo was born and brought up in a little village near Lisbon in Portugal.

Being interested in Asian philosophies since young, becoming a Yoga/Meditation instructor was just the right step to

Her experience in this field has awoken in her the audacity to express herself in a more blatant manner.

This is her first published work.

D1614669

Rute Paulo

# NOT JUST ANOTHER SPIRITUAL BOOK...

Leabharlanna Poiblí Chathair Baile Átha Cliath
Dublin City Public Libraries

## AUSTIN MACAULEY PUBLISHERS™
LONDON • CAMBRIDGE • NEW YORK • SHARJAH

A CIP catalogue record for this title is available from the British Library.

ISBN 9781788789813 (Paperback)
ISBN 9781788789820 (E-Book)

www.austinmacauley.com

First Published (2018)
Austin Macauley Publishers Ltd™
25 Canada Square
Canary Wharf
London
E14 5LQ

# Acknowledgements

I'm so grateful for all the struggles I went through in life, I felt pain, I felt despair, I wanted to give up, I lost hope and I wanted to disappear, but everything was worth it, because knowing myself, I could have been too passive and I wouldn't be here with you right now!

Thank you for buying this book.

Thank you for reading this book, I hope I could TOUCH you.

Thank you for allowing me to do something for myself and trying to make the SUN SHINE.

This book was a secret, however I would like to thank those who somehow contributed to the enrichment of these pages; the messengers can be anyone or anything.

Thank you Samuel Jun for being my companion, for respecting my wish and keeping your curiosity away.

Thank you, SR for all the support and for encouraging me to take action on writing this book.

Thank you to my lovely parents (A. Raimundo and M. Ascensão) and my two darlings, brother (Marco) and sister (Sara) for all your love and care.

A huge thank you to all the team at Austin Macauley Publishers for making all of this possible, for making this book a reality.

Of course, there is so much more to be said, so much to be discussed; these were just some of my thoughts that were boiling in my head waiting to be brought out and shared.

I humbly hope that I could be the butterfly who's back one day with more profound insights, more wise thoughts...

Thank You!!!

**Spirituality** = Decoding information; wise **Awareness**
**Meditation** = Method to achieve **Spirituality**
**Enlightenment** = Understand the **Laws of Nature**

# Note from the Author

Don't think that as you go through the pages of this book you will learn anything. These pages are just the words that I've chosen to express my wisdom I would like to say, but I'd rather say my feelings. ☺

These words might not change your life at all, but will definitely awaken in you the understanding towards the people around you who may think the same way as I do.

You don't have to agree to anything that I say, it's just my view points (which can change with time). Take with you what's for you and drop the rest.

It's not up to me to change your life, it's not my purpose and I don't want that responsibility.

The only thing I want to do is to TOUCH you, just that.

Touch and fly like a **butterfly**;

Love and fly and make your life more beautiful.

Loads of love and magical hugs,
Rute

I do not know anymore the meaning of to **be** and to be honest, I do not know if I ever did…

I do not know anymore the meaning of a **dream** and to be honest, I do not know if I ever had one…

Life has such **beautiful** things and I am very **fortunate** in many ways, but to be honest, I think that I am lost…

I'm no more than a robot…

I do not know anymore if I'm **happy** and to be honest I do not know if I ever was…

And now you may be thinking – *"If you're not happy, why don't you do something that could make you happy?"* – Because I do not know what I could do; I don't have a dream, I don't have a vision and my mission doesn't seem to me that grandiose.

I'm just tired of having many ideas and doing nothing about them.

I'm dying inside and to be honest, I do not know if I ever lived…

So, is this life? – F**k life!

Is this love? – F**k love!

Am I angry? – I don't know, maybe I am.

Sad? – Maybe I am, I don't know.

What I'm sure is that I am disappointed…

Yes, I am disappointed almost with everything in life.

Nothing is like as I dreamt. They're just illusions, sweet illusions.

People say that poets have the vein of sadness; I must have it too; the difference is that I don't write poems anymore.

I've read so many of the said spiritual books, so beautiful thoughts written in beautiful ways… but I realised they are just that… Beautiful!

They are these beautiful people who have the ability to write in a beautiful way what was written before, just with different words.

Hmm… you must be thinking that I am really unhappy, sad and angry…

Maybe! But I'm not frustrated. No, I'm not because despite my feelings, I still believe that **"It cannot rain forever, there will be a day that the sun will shine."**

I may be disappointed… lost…

And I do not know what to do; I just know that I **should** do something…

And here I am… with this book… looking for the **sun to shine.**

My book = my little secret.

I kept this book a secret, almost as if I was trying to protect myself from failure.

But why could it be a failure, if at the end of day, I just wanted to prove myself that actually I was able to do and finish something that could touch many people's lives. I do not know if it will touch your life, but at least there is a great trial and without trying I would never know…

It may sound very selfish, but I really want to know… even if it's a **failure**.

# Failure

– So, what is failure?
– How can it be a failure if you did not try?
– And if you try, how can it be failure?

## Noun: Failure
1. Lack of success.
2. **The neglect or omission of expected or required action**.
3. The action or state of not functioning (Google).

From the moment that you try is never a failure even if you don't succeed.

When there is dedication, when there is your best and more than anything else – when there is your courage – it's never a failure. Although you don't succeed, that's just the result of what you've tried. Perhaps there weren't the right conditions for it; perhaps you could have done better; perhaps it was not what people expected or perhaps you're just a bit ahead in time…

But did you really fail? – NO! What really matters is the whole package; your work, your will, what you've realised about yourself by going through the process of doing it. That's, in fact, the miracle; not the result itself. Did you ever think that there are so many things you probably didn't know about yourself, so many things that you had to overcome through the process of trying? There are fear and doubt (even when you're super confident of your abilities), there are errors and frustrations, but there are also will and hope, belief and faith.

So, how could it be a failure?

If you don't try, you will never know that deep inside you is a magical being who can detach himself from the results of his trials, and understand that are the results that can be subject of failure, but NEVER yourself.

Do not depend on what others may say to you, even when they say "Believe yourself" – beautiful words, but I would say: "Try and do your best and never compare yourself to others."

*"Don't listen to friends when the Friend inside you says 'Do this'."*

*~ Mahatma Gandhi ~*

*"Good, better, best. Never let it rest. 'Till your good is better and your better is best."*

*~ St. Jerome ~*

# Comparisons

*"Don't compare your life to others. You have no idea what
their journey is all about."*

*~ Anonymous ~*

When someone says something like this, "Oh, you are a good
person." You smile, but you cannot really internalise this
statement; in other words, it doesn't mean much to you and is
easily forgotten, because you do not enter the frequency of
feeling like the good person that you are.

The brain does not process the value of this information
(unless you have a great self-esteem).

So, we enter the world of comparisons.

When comparisons are made in relation to good situations
or people of good character and successful, or icons of the
society, we feel quite happy, but what makes us feel good
about it is not because we want to be exactly like that person
or because we may relate ourselves in some way; what really
makes the comment/comparison pleasing to us is the fact that
we are able to recognise its VALUE.

In the case of a negative comparison, it becomes more
complicated. Why?

Because the vibrations emitted from the first moment are
negative and because the great majority of us are most of the
time out of the vortex (spiral) of our **True Essence**. (Don't
you worry, I will come back to this thing of Vortex of True
Essence).

In fact, there is nothing that should be compared.

When we make comparisons, we enter in a world of
judgment; judgment conducts to conflict; conflict brings a

constant struggle, deception and expectation. And the worst part is that often this struggle comes from inside.

Things, situations, circumstances, people…are different!

Although the comparison can be very true and valid, it should not be done. We all have different experiences in life that lead to certain behaviours. Simple as that!

Be happy and let others be happy; no comparisons, no dramas.

Comparisons are in my humble opinion based on illusions. Illusions limit us and only let us see what we want to see. And often what we want to see is **not** real.

*"Things are as they are. Looking out into the universe at night, we make no comparisons between right and wrong stars nor between well and badly arranged constellations."*
*~ Alan Watts ~*

We all like to be unique; we all like to be special.

*"When you are content to be simply yourself and don't compare or compete, everyone will respect you."*
*~ Lao Tzu, Tao Te Ching ~*

Take a moment to **meditate** about it!

# Meditation

I would like to warn you that you might not agree with what I think of meditation and you don't have to…

**Meditation doesn't guarantee you Spirituality or Enlightenment.**
**Meditation is just a method, not a way.**

If you are a kind of a person who thinks that you shall wake up every day at a certain time to meditate and then struggle because it's hard to keep yourself awake or because you didn't sleep enough or because you can't get what you 'think' meditation may be; I'm sorry, but you're not doing any favours to yourself, you're just creating heaviness and tiredness.

It is true that you can master it, practice does it.

However, we only can reach the ownership of that state once we recognise our limitations.

Meditation does not necessarily have to be sitting crossed legs, hands resting on the knees and chanting (om). Meditation can be dynamic, dancing, singing; can be doing nothing or working hard; can be noisy or quiet; can be walking in the nature or simply breathing… and can be different every day.

**Meditation is a method, not a state!**
Meditation is not the absence of thought but focused thinking, which can take you into the non-physical dimension, the spiritual world. It is in this state that you may get the answers from deep within.

Feel yourself!

Meditation is that – feeling yourself, getting to know yourself, being with yourself and seeing yourself! The easiest meditation is the one that you focus on yourself, on the blessings of your life. There are many things that we don't really pay attention to. Feel your heart beat, how deep you breathe; visualise the good things in your life and be grateful for them – your loved ones, having a job, perhaps you have what you need to live life comfortably, the warmth of your house, the food that you're able to eat, the water to drink, the clothes you can wear and so many other things; or simply visualise and be grateful for everything that life is offering you to experience.

Sometimes those experiences can be painful and it is hard to keep a certain mind set, so maybe you'd like to try to look at those experiences as Steps or a Phase in your life. Instead of fighting against it, accept there is a reason and meditation can be the moment that you allow yourself to contemplate and feel the silence in order to understand it. When going through it, you may realise if there is anything you want to happen or change. You have to See yourself; and to see ourselves we need to judge*[1] our behaviours, patterns of thought, habits and tendencies. It's not easy, especially when we find something that we are not happy about or that we don't understand why is happening to us. 'Judging ourselves' is perhaps the hardest meditation; however, the best to begin with the change that you may be looking for.

There are people saying that they cannot meditate; well, that's not true, everybody has the ability to meditate – just feel yourself; just see yourself. Do not separate yourself from the act of meditating, do not focus on the image of how you think meditation should be and instead reflect about life and change/improve what you feel has to be changed/improved.

---

[1]**Judgement** (Please understand that the meaning of judgement is not always negative. Judgement also means discernment, acuity, cleverness, prudence and wisdom.)

*"You should be studying (life lessons) all the time and improve."*

*~ Master Jinjung ~*

Only when you really SEE yourself, you can realise what Steps life is and has been offering you to help you to grow into the person that you truly are and to fulfil the mission of your life – a person who lives life with great respect to himself and others, a person who honours nature and a person who's humble enough to understand and accept **that everything in nature is in constant mutation including oneself.**

Let meditation happen naturally without forcing anything, accept there are times that you cannot go that deep; accept (not engaging) when there are thoughts disturbing; accept the images, the words, the feelings that are coming to you. Often it feels like as if you are imagining things, as if you're dreaming, and sometimes you may feel as if you're in another world. And if the question comes to you – "Is that for real? Did I really feel/see/hear anything or was it my imagination?" The answer is again – ACCEPT! Accept that sometimes it's better than others, accept that sometimes you cannot stop thinking and sometimes it's just too unreal. Once you accept it, you are on the right path and that is called **growth**.

# Growth

*"The key to growth is the introduction of higher dimensions of consciousness into our awareness."*

*~ Lao Tzu ~*

Growth is a deeper understanding of what we already know.

We all came to this world with some kind of information package and we are here to upgrade ourselves, it's almost like doing a PhD, so our soul gets another degree and our spirit gets a lighter energy.

Sometimes I feel there's no point to discuss Soul and Spirit… because there is no exact explanation about it.

Perhaps the point is living your life in the best way that you can.

I know what you are thinking: *"Yeah right, that we already know,"* I would think the same if I was hearing that, but what I mean is: there were so many philosophers, spiritual teachers and researchers and no one was able to explain anything – perhaps we don't need it… we are so focused on trying to understand and define what Soul and Spirit could be when we're actually missing out what we should really focus on, which is being happy.

Think about – Do you really think much about Soul if you're happy?

The situations in life that we go through from time to time are Steps of Life (not tests); if we understand its meaning we get closer to the answers we are looking for, each of those Steps give us the possibility of getting another degree (a Soul degree).

No one says it will be easy though, sometimes it is quite painful, sometimes it hurts so much that you want to give up, sometimes you feel so angry and you will be asking, "What is the purpose of this f*****g life?", sometimes you feel despair like a cancer in your life...

And when you hear this kind of stuff – "you'll get there"; "everything happens for a reason"; "you can do this"; "you're stronger than you think you are" – again, it feels like crap, all crap. Of course, the one who said it just wants you to feel that they are there for you (which has to be appreciated), but what can they do if there is a lesson for you?

As mentioned before, among the years I've been reading quite a lot of self-development books which I found very helpful... Probably you did it too...

But did you realise that it seems to work just for a little while and then you lose motivation?

That happens because in spite of you trying to focus on the positive side, you still have to work on the problem, otherwise everything seems to come back again and over again.

Did you ever try to do a 'brain storm' with yourself or with the help of a friend?

Before blaming others or yourself, before putting yourself down or exploding at others, think what could be the reason to explain what you're going through in Life.

There are some many other examples that we could look at, but these two might be enough for you to have a rough idea of what I mean.

**Example 1:** *For sure you have experienced situations where you felt that you shouldn't do something but anyway you did it and then ended up feeling frustrated or upset because deep inside you knew you shouldn't have done it. If you can understand what you have done 'wrong', although it was with good intention, you will become aware when a similar situation comes to you and prevents you from going through it again.*

**Example 2:** *Another situation that happens quite often is not saying what you really think (whatever the reason; sometimes it's because you want to avoid conflict or whenever you're trying to make your point you're just bashed or the people involved tend to distort whatever you're trying to say or because you don't know how to express yourself or because you simply lost the motivation to speak out what's in your chest). Although the reason could be very strong, won't make the situation go away by itself, it will keep coming to you until you sort it out, no matter how good a person you may be or how much you're trying to keep the harmony between you and others. It's important that you speak out, it takes a lot of effort at first, but you have to do it otherwise you will feel that you're banging your head on the wall at all times and you don't want that to continue happening in your life.*

Similar problems or situations which can create the similar harsh feelings that you already experienced, will appear until you work out your tendencies or habits. Once you 'cook' yourself, another Step will come (step not test) for you to grow higher.

Try to think this way – if there is a step, better to be a new one to help you get out of the closet, out of the comfortable zone rather than the same old issue which is not taking you anywhere and making you feel that your life is worthless. Give yourself permission to grow.

**Among time and self-work, you will start seeing what Soul could be, its importance and meaning. Like a mathematical equation, what seems abstract at first will start eventually making more sense, meaning the more you understand the language of your soul and its information, the higher is the degree and the lighter the Spirit becomes.**

# Spirituality

To be spiritual, you don't necessarily need to go to a retreat centre or temple in India or Thailand; if you have the opportunity – go for it and enjoy yourself, but don't be sorry if you for some reason cannot make it. Don't take this as criticism.

I, myself, also had that fantasy of going to Tibet as if that could be the answer for all the deep questions that I had/have. I still would like to go, but now without the illusion of acquiring some kind of spiritual powers.

Of course, you won't be the same person after a deep experience independently of what you may achieve in that retreat. Experience is an add up in your Life, but doesn't mean that you will turn into an enlightened master.

It's a trend to think that all the enlightened people went to a mountain or monastery and magically turned into a special person. If it was just like that, wouldn't it be so lovely?

Please be aware that the effect of seclusion may not stay forever or it may become what I call the spiritual arrogance – a common mistake after a spiritual training. You think you know it all, the true truth; you think that you're very open-minded and very sensitive, spiritually speaking, but when experiencing a different way of energy work – you judge and compare and try to show that you know better. Or you can become spiritually disturbed, meaning that you may become extremely sensitive to non-physical manifestations and you do not know how to deal with it.

Do not think that I'm against spiritual trainings or retreats, not at all; I just don't want you to fall into an illusion. In fact, I would like to encourage you to do it. You can experience such beautiful things as well as finding more about your own journey and who knows even getting a Soul degree.

I think that the best way or at least the safest way for a spiritual journey is developing and refining your awareness in relation to the feeling of **Energy**. It may feel a bit conceptual, but is indeed very simple, because energy is natural in all of us. You can stimulate your sensitivity by practicing energy work such as Yoga, Qigong or any activity where you are mindful.

We often forget the factor – Energy.

**Energy is invisible but always present.**

Energy is the bridge between the physical and non-physical worlds, between your body and your Soul. You just need to be conscious of what it means/feels to you. It's not something that you can acknowledge by academic understanding but acknowledging by feeling.

Please note, the sensation of energy is changeable and even unpredictable because everything is cyclical. Life is cyclical, Nature is cyclical, even breathing is cyclical – you can not only breathe in, you have to breathe out. And sometimes you feel better breathing in and filling up your chest with fresh air and sometimes you prefer the sensation of breathing out and letting go.

When I was younger, I thought that to be spiritual would be learning about the invisible, the unknown, the occult; today I realised that being spiritual is all about real life. That's why souls come for a degree in this world; if everything was so magical up there, in that other dimension, why would souls take a journey in a form of a human body?

Spirituality is about growth. Growth is about understanding the Steps of Life. Steps of Life are struggles, strives, endeavours. Sometimes we succeed and sometimes it's very frustrating. Exactly like breathing we need both; you cannot just breathe in, you cannot just breathe out. In the Steps of Life we can't only succeed, we also have to struggle. But nothing is fruitless!

**Without struggle, there is no Growth and without Growth there is no Spirituality.**

And this is why I say most of the spiritual books that we read every now and then are just beautiful words. In these books, everything is so great and magical, everything seems so easy and miraculous... and what about the tough times? What about the lack of energy to overcome those times? What about what we actually need to understand/learn/fix? What about real life?

I do agree that reading those beautiful words encourages us, something resonates with us which can help going through the shaking times of life. We all came to this world with some kind of package and in order to SEE what package is that, we need to get the shaking time. Otherwise most of us will become too passive, waiting for miracles to happen out of nothing.

Miracles do happen, but only if you're ready. No matter if you try your best to attract all the fortune into your life, no matter if you are visualising and trying to feel as if it's your reality, no matter if you drank the magic potion; it only matters if you're ready for whatever you ask for. We all have wishes and desires and it is OK trying to be positive and believe hard something good is going to happen, but we never question if we are ready for it.

*E.g. you dream of a beach house in Polynesian Islands and you somehow get it, and then? Are you ready to maintain the house so far away from where you live? Do you have enough money to fly often so you can enjoy the house? – Look, this is just an example, but I think you know what I mean. Yes, sometimes we get what we want, but if we're not ready we also get what we don't want. Another example is winning the lottery, most of us speak out loud, "If I win the lottery, oh gosh, what I would do?" – We all kind of day-dream about it but it often happens that the lucky one doesn't really manage well all that money and even says he/she was happier when they didn't have that money.*

So, in short, if you are ready, the **real miracles** will happen.

Perhaps you are now asking yourself – "How do I know if I am ready?" The language that the spiritual books utilise would be more likely – "The answer is within yourself!" which is TRUE. The problem is how we can recognise the so told answers. How can we be sure of the answers? How do we know if it is real or fruit of our imagination? How can we go within ourselves and get the right answer?

How can I know? – The answer is within yourself.

Sorry, I was being naughty.

I wish I could be 100% sure, but I am not. However, this is what I think it is the meaning of finding the answer within ourselves:

∞   Questioning.

It's important that you keep questioning yourself. Ask if it is really what you want; how happy, excited, anxious or afraid are you just by thinking of it. Is it really worth it? If you get what you think you want, that's it? And then what will you do? Will it change your life so much? Are you ready to cope with that change and its consequences?

∞   Meditation.

Meditation is perhaps the best method to go inside by questioning ourselves of what we want/need/ what is best (this is one of the reasons that meditation can be sometimes very noisy, non-stop thinking and very confusing; but that's the process in progression). Meditation is giving a chance to the intuitive side of yours, it's feeling the sensations of your body as the answers start arising. Meditation may not bring all the answers at once as you may need to break with your resistance and/or stubbornness. The process may take longer than you wish, but that's 'the price' to pay for trying to go deeper within. Sometimes, it may feel dark or something like a code and you cannot understand it until you decipher the code. Be patient, it's almost like learning a foreign language, starting from the basics until you could formulate a sentence.

∞ Repetitive thoughts or feelings.
You start to think about a certain subject within the same pattern, having the same kind of feelings. At a certain stage even your behaviour starts to be according to those feelings *(e.g. you are living in a foreign country and you're going to a home decoration shop and like something there but then you start thinking better not buy anything in case you have to move away, better not accumulate too much stuff).* The decision might not be made yet, but unconsciously you start behaving as if so. Another example is when you realise that you're telling people what, in fact, you should be doing. *(This has happened to me, I kept saying to people – "You should write that down" – I was saying this to many people in the most different circumstances, until I understood that I was the one who should be doing that. And here I am).*

∞ Be attentive to the gentle signs that Nature offers you. Sometimes, the angels are the people around us, who don't necessarily have to have any kind of relationship with you. The messages are not always straight forward and may feel like nothing to do with you; could be something that you witness; could be a quote that you read in a book or magazine. Could be anything! Now, these signs are coming to you when there is some work already done, because being spiritual is having the ability to go inside and not expecting that Nature will do the homework for you. These signs are more like a <u>confirmation</u> to what you already know somehow, a help for you to trust yourself, for you to be surer of your decision.

∞ Excitement or anxiety.

Feel your body; you may feel something such as a gentle vibration inside out. The physical sensations are quite important. Just following signs (from the outside) can be very tricky and very brainy. So, try to feel more than analysing. You may have different sensations in your chest. You may feel some tightness and that could mean it's not the right thing for you; it may be the right thing for you but you're afraid of it and its consequences; you aren't ready; or simply you've entered the world of the 'buts and ifs'. On the other hand, you may feel excited and happy when thinking or meditating about something. You start to make plans in your head. By going through some sort of a situation you are happy about, you 'see' yourself experiencing it in the environment that you're day-dreaming of and you may experience talking to yourself out loud. (Confess – you're doing it (talking to yourself) more often than you want to say, isn't it? And more so when you have something that's shaking you, no matter if in negative or positive way).

That's why I mentioned meditation – to peel off the layers; the more you keep questioning yourself, the more layers you get rid of.

*"You go through countless layers over long period of time and maybe shed a few tears along the way; you are peeling off the many layers of you to find YOURSELF."*

(Anonymous)

Feeling happy and excited doesn't always signify that you're doing the right thing or that's right for you. In my point of view, sometimes that happiness is just an illusion, you think you are creating or solving something but perhaps you're just trying to do it quickly or missing out what's the truth of the situation and you decide to use a 'plaster' which is temporary and ephemeral; in order to feel that excitement, you need to be crystal clear independently of the way or steps to take as these you can work on later.

*E.g. – You want A but you get B instead, because B will do for the time-being BUT it's not what you really wanted. So, you're happy for some time, but deep inside you know that wasn't exactly what you wanted, you probably could wait a bit longer and prepare better and get A.*

It also may feel more confusing or that you're adding up layers instead – but remember – "Every cloud has a silver lining." – which in this case means that even when it feels dark and heavy, it's not necessarily a bad sign, you need to be patient to yourself because sometimes it happens slowly and very softly; I think the best is preparing well, it's getting ready for.

And this, my friend, is for me part of what I understand of spirituality.

To obtain spirituality you don't need to practice Tummo Meditation[2]* or self-flagellation[3]** (unless you want to, we all have different ways to get in touch with ourselves), you

---

[2] **Tummo    Meditation**    *Tummo* (Tibetan: *gtum-mo*; Sanskrit: *caṇḍālī*) is a form of breathing. The purpose of tummo is to gain control over body processes during the completion stage of 'highest yoga tantra' (Anuttarayoga Tantra) or Anuyoga. (Wikipedia)

[3] ** **Self-flagellation** The action of flogging oneself, especially as a form of religious discipline. Excessive criticism of oneself. (Google)

need to **be aware** of the informative gifts presented to you (signs, allies and acquaintances; gut feelings, intuition and insights), **be wise in your choices** (please note that, wise choices do not prevent you from pain and suffering).

Spirituality is becoming conscious of the information at the level of non-physical world, it's the awareness of what we cannot control but has indeed a great influence on us and the same time due to our choices we also can influence it (the non-physical world) immensely, regardless of how **conscious** you are of it. So, be wise in your choices.

# Steps of Life

You might have realised already that I am naming 'Steps of Life' or simply 'Steps' to what normally people would denominate life lessons or tests. That's because the way I see it is really as a step not as a test or lesson (although sometimes I use these words for better understanding when interacting with others).

It's almost like being at school (basing myself on the old system of education where you are approved or not, depending on how well you did on the different subjects). You keep going on in certain way in Life until you realise what you have to learn with it. Until then, it may feel like that your life is just going around and around, and not taking you anywhere, making you feel stuck and often demotivated or even depressed or burned out…

**Example 1:** *A man or a woman who keeps having new partners and going through similar kind of relationship.*

**Example 2**: *A person having similar professional situations despite of the change of bosses or even jobs.*

It's a MUST to understand what the step is/was all about? But up to here you've already understood, right?

– So why am I calling it steps and not lessons or tests?

Thinking of tests feels to me complicated and you may succeed or fail and if you fail you might start to see yourself as victim. And lessons feel like – if you do well, great! But if not, you feel as if you're dull (just banging with your head).

Maybe I am too lazy thinking this way but to me thinking in terms of steps feel lighter and simpler. Another word that I like to use is **Phase**, again feels lighter and simpler.

I don't want you to simply agree with me; I want you to try to feel what I mean. Please try saying to yourself or imagining that someone is telling you this: "So, do you think that you've learnt anything this time with this situation?" or "What do you think you need to learn out of this?" or "Another test… why me?" or "Where can I get if my life is full of tests from everywhere?" And think a little bit longer and say: "Well, I think I am going through another phase of my life, what's this step all about? Or "Is this situation another step of Life?"

How do you feel about it? Probably you don't see a great difference and that's alright, but let me keep this point of view (at least for time being – yes, because everything is subject of mutation, including myself).

However, whether it's a Phase or a Step of Life doesn't mean it becomes easier, in fact requires loads of patience and study. So do not get lazy! ☺

And by the way, you are not a **victim** of anything!

# Issued

Branch: Dublin City Dolphin's Barn
Date:   11/09/2023      Time:    3:19 PI
Name:   Kearney, Patrick

| ITEM(S) | DUE DAT |
| --- | --- |
| Tracing your Irish family...<br>XCPL0000701549 | 02 Oct 202 |
| Not just another spiritual...<br>XCPL9000084608 | 02 Oct 202 |

Your current loan(s): 2
Your current reservation(s): 0
Your current active request(s): 0

To renew your items please log onto My
Account at https://dublincity.spydus.i

Thank you for using your local library

# Victim Behaviour and Destiny

*"When someone beats a rug, the blows are not against the rug, but against the dust in it."*

~ *Rumi* ~

We all feel somehow to be victims of the different situations in life and it is so much easier to see it in that way. However, the truth is: we are not victims of anything. Seeing ourselves as victims is a **learnt behaviour,** excusing ourselves as if going through some condition pre-established in life, in one word – Destiny.

*"Only 30% is what we understand as destiny; 70% is your own creation."*

~ *Master Jinjung* ~

The only destiny that we have pre-established is death, nothing else. Otherwise, what would we come to do in this world? Destiny is not a dictator. Destiny is just another excuse for not making the necessary changes in life.

So, no point saying things in life are going in a certain way because of this or that situation, because of this or that person. No, it's no point because it's not true. Life is as it is, because you did not see the Step and what you had to understand with it. Perhaps you didn't understand because you couldn't see what it was or because it felt too much at that time, maybe you weren't ready; perhaps you didn't know any better or you didn't want to care about it or perhaps you couldn't simply let go.

**It's nothing to be blamed, but it's not to be ignored either.**

Sometimes it's just habits and sometimes you don't really want to accept there is something to work in yourself and sometimes it's a matter of communication (not only between you and others but with yourself). People tend to blame what's around for the misunderstandings or lapses in their lives. It is quite common to explain the lack of communication between one another with the external stimulations. **We cannot only look outside of us for a reason**, if something has to change, do not expect that to happen from others, don't look for excuses.

I really find it hard to agree with some spiritual leaders who say that our reality is create by us, but… I kind of agree somehow… there is a certain truth in it.

Think about:

**Reality is a formula of the way we think and also how well we go through the Steps in life.**

Don't you tend to act, think and behave within a certain pattern?

– I do, everybody does until one of those Steps come to shake us. And then either you clear it up properly, I mean you fully 'cook' the Step that you're going through or you just wipe it out. If you just wipe it out and anyway you feel good – hello, it will happen again! I'm afraid so! We need to clear all out in order to fulfil our life, wiping is not enough, is temporary and is an illusion.

**It's the process of clearing that helps us to realise our own potential and value.**

So, do we create our reality?

Yes and No.

– Yes, **our actions should be the reflection of our original energy**.

If you aren't able to bring up that energy, you will start attracting what you don't want, your actions are not matching with your genuineness.

You are the only one who can clear, understand, fix and overcome the Step; so, if you don't do it, no one can do that for you, independently of having others involved would be like loose ends left swinging, holding you back for not resembling with your natural *vibrational frequency[4].

– No, because you are NOT the only one deciding. And no, I'm not talking about others, I'm talking about a spiritual level that is quite present in our Life although silent. To understand this non-visible world can be complicated and you need to be sensitive to it. The best way to be more aware of this influence is to enhance your intuition.

That's why you might feel you need help and that's OK, do not hesitate to ask for help. That's not a sign of weakness, it's in fact being courageous – recognising that there is some limitation in overcoming the Step reveals that you are working on it and looking for the 'little piece of the puzzle' that's missing, however it's all in your hands, don't rely on others, expecting them to have answers neglecting your own intuition, expecting them to do homework for you neglecting your own responsibility.

**Regarding your life is all your responsibility.**

And this is the reason you cannot see yourself as a victim of anything even when you think others are affecting your life. When that happens is of course more difficult, you may have to take into account what others may think or how would they behave in relation to the situation. It is very tricky and I must confess that I am struggling a lot with it. I wish to have an answer for you right now, but is something I am still working on (who knows if my next book is about this subject – change our vibrational frequency, tie the loose ends). I am pretty good at helping others analysing the situation and get a more

---

[4] * *For better understanding of Vibrational Frequency: The Universal-Energy-of **Frequency** and **Vibration**.     Everything **Vibrates**: This Universal Law states that everything in the Universe moves and **vibrates** – everything is vibrating at one speed or another. Nothing rests. Everything you see around you is vibrating at one **frequency** or another and so are you.(Google)*

peaceful way to see a neutral point of view (not as good regarding myself, though, ha–ha–ha but not funny ha–ha ☺).

I used to say whatever you're going through in life has two sides (like a coin), your version and the other person's version; until one day a great friend of mine (SR) told me there is always three versions and I realised that I was very much black and white, very much Yin and Yang, so now I make her words mine: **"There is what you see and there is what the other person sees and the most important – there is what the situation truly is!"**

As you can see the third perspective is, in fact, a non-physical perspective.

*"God writes spiritual mysteries on our hearts, where they wait silently for discovery."*

*~ Rumi ~*

What I am trying to do now is stepping back and assessing the situation from a different perspective, having everything into account as if I am peeling off the various layers of the onion, but the onion makes you cry and what you see can be quite blurry; so it can be hard to get the right outcome and sometimes the right outcome can be painful. But as I said previously, I am working on this subject, still a lot of trial and error, which means don't be desperate if you don't feel that you're managing well this matter – You're not alone!

I know this doesn't comfort you much, but the truth is – you are not a victim, you are in a **process of growth and discovery** which implicates various Steps.

Remember these Steps can turn into blessings and not accepting those Steps can cause retardation of your Self-development; however, it will always be your **choice**.

# Mission

Often people think of Mission as something grandiose, majestic, almost like the development of a supernatural power, something that changes people's lives, something BIG...

Mission is not like that for everybody... if every one of us had such a grandiose mission, it would be like as if everybody in the world had the same profession. And if we all had the same profession, how could we survive? That's exactly the same regarding the mission of each one of us.

*"Not all of us can do great things. But we can do small things with great love."*

~ *Mother Teresa* ~

There are no more or less important missions.

No matter if your mission is to be someone like Mahatma Gandhi or Mother Teresa of Calcutta; or someone who seems having no importance in the world – everybody is as important and precious.

Mission could be simply being present for others, listening, sharing your ability to care and love or making others smile... could be studying, could be changing a concept in Physics or Psychology.

And could be (you're not going to like this) driving others crazy or even killing. I also don't want to agree with this, but I've heard some teachings in relation to this matter which makes sense. This teacher says it has to do with the contradictions created by the humanity. However, I'd rather not get into much detail until I 'digest' this information properly.

If you are pursuing something big although you have no idea of what that could be, Stop and pay attention to your talents (maybe the dormant ones, the ones in the back of your mind), start giving value to what you're offering of yourself.

E.g. I used to say that people may think that I'm Mother Teresa, because since young age, people were coming to me to talk about their problems. I felt sometimes that I had some kind of magnet that attracted people to me. Then I started to feel overwhelmed; I would be thinking of people and their problems. Tried to pray for all of them but the list was becoming too extensive and I've just got too lazy to do so. But I couldn't stop myself from feeling sympathy for others (I did stop saying that I'd pray for them, just in case I forget or didn't feel like doing it).

Among the years, I always wanted to make the difference in the world, so I learnt how to feel for people but at the same time detach from their issue. Then, a bigger problem appeared – people expect me to say something, they expect me to give them answers, the right answers, which I don't always have… And even if I had it, it's not always up to me to say it (it would be like someone telling you the end of a book before you reading it), which means it's their responsibility to find out… I'm not a fortune teller! And everything is subject to change, the probabilities are variable, depending on how one behaves in relation to the situation, the time and space.

Now (just for curiosity, perhaps you have similar situations and this helps me, it might help you too), what I do is: I might not say much while the person is talking to me and allow myself to feel and come back to the person later on.

Ah… and if I say to someone, "I pray for you", I really pray though ☺.

But with all this conversation you might be asking, "Why is she saying all of this stuff?" or "So what?" The reason is that I never saw what I mentioned above about myself as something special, pompous, big, because it really felt like nothing, but listening, treating ailment is my talent; a talent which could become even bigger.

And this small big talent is part of my mission despite of the way I see it.

So, are you really paying attention to your talents?

Remember, being grandiose doesn't happen just like that; **being grandiose is the accumulation of small feats.**

Normally, big missions are synonymous of big pain (this is my feeling), but no matter how difficult it could be; don't let your **fears** put you down… Remember your **Mission**, the more you work on it the happier you will be.

Gandhi suffered a lot until he died…

Mother Teresa of Calcutta suffered a lot and never felt complete…

Jesus suffered a lot, was killed and never fully understood…

But **they never gave up**…

*"Out of suffering have emerged the strongest souls; the most massive characters are seared with scars."*
~ *Kahlil Gibran* ~

SO, are you working on your mission?

*"To be great, be whole;*
*Exclude nothing, exaggerate nothing that is not you.*
*Be whole in everything. Put all you are*
*Into the smallest thing you do.*
*So, in each lake, the moon shines with splendour*
*Because it blooms up above."*
~ *Fernando Pessoa* ~
*(Poems of Fernando Pessoa)*

# Fear

It is one of the highest frequencies, but in the opposite direction. Meaning that the frequency of fear is very strong, so strong that it distances us greatly from the Origin (Zero Point).

And the question is: What do you do to confront/deal with this fear?

Unfortunately, what I can say is that it all depends on what you choose.

Fear does not often, if not always, let you see what is beyond; even when you're making a great effort to overcome that fear. Images occur to you and those images or sensations are projections of the brain that anticipate feelings in you such as anguish, failure, impotence, inferiority, etc. There is a visualisation of the situation that has not yet happened and your body reacts, causing you to loosen up, stop and eventually step back. Then come the feelings of frustration and melancholy, you start to believe you're not able to and you conform yourself with the idea of 'I tried, but I didn't make it', going backwards even further than the zero-point, entering a vicious cycle without major changes.

It is important to note that this cycle is not always the result of fear. Fear may be present, but there are often other constraints such as lack of motivation, information you may have about the subject, or because you've tried various times without succeeding, allowing the projections of failure and disguise taking over your courage, or simply you do not believe to be possible.

*"I've learned that fear limits you and your vision. It serves as blinders to what may be just a few steps down the road for you. The journey is valuable, but believing in your talents, your abilities, and your self-worth can empower you to walk down an even brighter path.*
*Transforming fear into freedom – how great is that?"*
*~ Soledad O'Brien ~*

*"I learned that courage was not the absence of fear, but the triumph over it. The brave man is not he who does not feel afraid, but he who conquers that fear."*
*~ Nelson Mandela ~*

# Negative Emotions

Humans are full of good, bad or so/so feelings, but this everyone knows…

Having negative emotions can be a powerful experience.

*"Some emotions, like happiness and excitement, light us up – while others like frustration and anger can engulf us in a negative mood. <u>Emotions are powerful tools that allow us to experience the highs and lows of life and give us important intuitive clues.</u>*

*We all want to experience joy, happiness, excitement, and peace more frequently than sadness, frustration, fear, or anger. But we are human beings and life, as we all know, is a roller coaster of emotions.*

<u>*Negative feelings are inevitable*</u>*"*

*(The Power of Negative Emotions by Michael Forman –* https://wanderlust.com*)*

Now-a-days, it's quite fashionable to be 'spiritual' and loads of people like to think of themselves as very wise and so on and that's a good thing, but being spiritual doesn't mean that everything is 'peace and love'. When people enter a more spiritual world, the tendency is to think that they should not have the so-called negative emotions; as spiritual-beings they should be in control, they should be 'above' such feelings.

I have a friend who's not religious at all and even though sometimes asks – "Do you think that Jesus would get angry?" – I really think that the answer is, "Of course!" – He was also going through his own journey, he was also in a learning process exactly like each one of us.

The Enlightenment happens when you sort out your own contradictions and that's why having negative emotions/feelings can be a powerful experience and full of meaning.

Therefore, the question – "How can you know if what you feel is good, if you do not know what it feels like to be bad and vice versa?" – seems to me very reasonable.

E.g.:
- Rage

How can you know what serenity is if you haven't felt anger/fury?
You do not know!
Rage, anger is also energy and with a great power too. Having these feelings is not to harm others or yourself but to realise the strong force that you are able to move from inside out.
- Fear

How do you know what your limits are if you do not feel fear?
You do not know!

- Acceptance

How do you know what might be acceptable if you do not know what might be unacceptable to you?
You do not know!
Just be aware that sometimes we may confuse what feels unacceptable with **stubbornness**.

- Hate

How can you know what real love is if you never experience dislike and hate?
You do not know!

- Doubt

How do you know what seems right or wrong to you if you do not question?

You do not know!

Is important to doubt and question, not falling into a blind-knowledge or some sort of illusion. Is important to question yourself if it feels right to you in order to give a chance to your intuitive feelings. <u>Doubting is not to put yourself down but to stimulate your intuition</u>.

And now probably you're saying that you are confused... and asking, "So having bad feelings is good?" – I would say: "Yes!"

– Because?

– Because it's the way to realise the value of the good things that happen to you, that's surrounding you. For what you define as good to have more impact on your life; in other words, appreciate the blessings of your life.

Did it never happen to you that you went through certain situations in life that were sometimes extreme and difficult; but now that you look back and reflect, you feel that there was evolution? That made you see what you haven't seen before? That helped you encounter an unknown reality in yourself that can turn out being great talents or dormant vocations?

*"In the middle of the difficulty lies the opportunity."*
*~ Albert Einstein ~*

Have you ever thought that what can seem reasonable to you might not be to others or vice versa?

Yes, I know that my question is a very simple question, but what I want to point out here is: what is considered a bad feeling may possibly be good, it all depends on the frequency you vibrate. Which means that all depends on your mood. Your mood creates a welter and you see things through it; if you're in a good mood, things become much more positive than if you're in a bad mood. OK, OK, I know, you already know this, but do you really know it, did you really think about it?

However, this welter or sift can also be neutral. Being neutral means seeing things as they really are (is a matter of training yourself).

This is a kind of allegory so you can understand a little better: think of the painting of Mona Lisa by Leonardo da Vinci – is she smiling? Is she not smiling? Or is she smiling but not smiling? The way you see is affected by the way you're feeling, so your emotions have a great impact on the way you filter things and as a result the vibrational frequency is subject to constant variations. These vibrational frequencies may continue to resonate in you, becoming stronger and stronger and to change that, you might like to start from identifying it, accepting it and even being grateful, because at that moment you have the opportunity to choose to see what really has or makes sense to you; encouraging you to make a decision; motivating you to take action and eventually dropping off those filters – often the reason for many problems in the relationship with others.

The moment of choice has in the invisible or energetic (if you prefer) world a tremendous power, although we cannot see it, although in our human eyes, it feels like nothing.

In short, often what may seem bad at first sight can be very beneficial, it may be almost a miracle, because it may be the turnaround you need to have in your life, to evolve, to make your life more meaningful.

*"It is a mistake to interfere with this movement of feeling. It is more appropriate to recognize that this emotion belongs more to your clay than to your mind. It is wise to let this weather of feeling pass; it is on its way elsewhere. We so easily forget that our clay has a memory which preceded our minds, a life of its own before it took our present form."*
*~ John O'Donohue ~*
*(Anam Cara, A Book of Celtic Wisdom)*

# Recognition

There are many teachers alleging that we should get rid of the need of recognition.

It is true that you shall not depending on that need too much as well as rely on how well recognised you will be, however recognition for what you are and what you do is important to a certain extent. It is a good feeling when you're recognised for the kind of person that you may be; it is good to be recognised when you perform at studies/work in a successful way.

It's good to be recognised and that's it!

Being recognised helps you to feel appreciated and see yourself with greater value and potential, makes you feel motivated and encourages you to work hard in whatever you may be doing.

So, being recognised feels good and that's it!

The problem emerges when you switch from the feeling good of being appreciated to the need and in many cases the greed for recognition. That's dependence!

Depending on recognition from others is a poisonous relationship between you and YOU. Because 'you' will become a slave of what others may think, influencing the way you think, behave and act; you will become a pleaser, nothing else.

You may feel good and happy for a while, but be aware that's a fake happiness. At a certain stage of your life, you'll feel tired, drained and with a big gap in you; you will feel that you've been giving too much of yourself in detriment of Yourself and that's painful.

You don't need to be a Pleasing Machine to be recognised; the 'YOU' wants you to explore your creativity, vocation and strengths. You just need to be assertive and wise.

Being assertive and wise means:
- You're aware of your potential, but humble to accept a change
- You're good but you don't need to keep proving that, although you can always be better
- Accept there will be critics and believe some of those can be very constructive
- Be open to listen what others may have to say but without neglecting your own value
- Don't be too hard on yourself but hard enough to do the right thing

Some of the reasons that can cause a greater need of recognition from others is the hardship that you impose on yourself either because you're a perfectionist or you're not sure of yourself and of course – fear. If this is your case, rather than putting yourself down, try to understand the cause, there are many factors that can contribute to the lack of confidence and diffidence.

Do not expect to be recognised at all the times even when you think that you've done your best. People perceive things in different ways.

E.g. I used to teach yoga and sometimes I thought I'd done a great class but at the end I had no feedback at all, and sometimes I thought my class wasn't anything special but I received great feedback.

I like to think that period of non-recognition, stand-by or even critical time, is the preparation for another Step/Phase. Sometimes, it's a challenge that is presented, giving us the chance to see our limitations and fears, to work on them and recognise our **True Essence**.

*"Whatever you do will be insignificant, but it is very
important that you do it."*

*~ Mahatma Gandhi ~*

# Vortex of True Essence

As I mentioned (in the chapter – Comparisons), I would get back to you about this story of Vortex of True Essence. Otherwise, it would be one more of those expressions to put into the collection of the beautiful concepts…

True Essence is what you truly are. And what you truly are is not what you may think you are. You are a combination of egos, memories and experiences.

You are living in a **pretending world** and most of you are NOT being **YOU** 95% of the time.

You may think that you're authentic, but the truth is that you're **wearing a mask** and believe me – you have many.

When you're meeting your boss, for example, you want to give a good impression, you want to pass an image of you being dynamic, enthusiastic and intelligent; when meeting college mates, after not seeing them for some time, it is almost automatic that you try to behave as quite successful and doing well in life; you're going out with friends and you try to be funny and indulgent, although it might not exactly be what you really want to do; you're dating someone and you want to impress, you want the person to think of you as someone special (whatever special may mean to you); you try to look pretty and younger, expecting to get attention and praise from the other. And there are also the cases of the attention seekers (these ones, I confess I have no patience at all for), the 'poor me, poor me' people, who consciously or unconsciously try to attract the others attention by passing an image of themselves as being sicker than they really are; poor and miserable; having difficulties in life, more than anyone else;

the drama-people, who tend to 'make a storm in a glass of water'.

This is not a criticism though, we all do it somehow; some more than others, some less; some in one way or some in another; because we are too dependent of what image others may have about us, what they think and so on. It's almost as if we see ourselves through the eyes of the others and this is a very serious problem, that leads us to pretend to be someone we're not and which is a mere image, like a hologram.

This is Self-Corruption! And this corruption prevents us from seeing our real Essence.

The Vortex of our True Essence is a spiral of energy composed by the information of your past lives, DNA and the desire of your soul's mission in the present life. I do not believe that we can be completely out of the Vortex, otherwise we would be already in the other dimension. So, there is hope, which means that we can recognise up to a certain extent (at least 5%) some beauty, ability and power in us; truly! It's just not enough for us to prevail. We need to increase this percentage in relation to the length of time that we ARE ourselves.

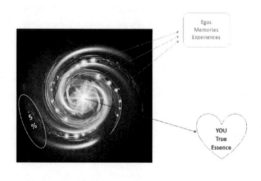

How?
**Enlightenment** is the answer.

# Enlightenment

Enlightenment doesn't happen from one moment to another.

Enlightenment is the ability to put into practice the understanding of the Steps of Life.

Being enlightened is different from being wise.

You can be a paragon of virtues on a particular matter and at the same time being a complete crap regarding different subjects; meaning that you're not an enlightened master just because of the fact that you got the insight in relation to certain aspects of life; that's a process and acquired knowledge through time and experiential livingness.

Whilst being wise is a knowing by knowing, is some kind of information which is somehow stronger than intuition, coming from a special and pure source; is so to speak a divine source of information.

There are people who brought with them a great package of information, knowledge and serenity; it's amazing listening to them. They have a source of information that they can filter by quieting and connecting in deeper way with themselves as if they activate a mechanism of clarity, finding the right words for the moment.

We weren't all born like that but I believe we all have the chance to awaken to the insights of life. There will always be chances for you to look at situations, problems and yourself from a different perspective if you're willing to. It is as if you could fly high into the white and soft clouds, looking down and everything seems so small and sometimes insignificant; is allowing yourself to get detached from life and as you keep flying high and the clouds become even brighter, your eyes may become heavier and heavier and although you may not keep your eyes open any longer but you still can see, you can see by feeling. It is when you see by feeling that you awaken the ability to see things as they really are and not as you think they may be. You will be blessed by Nature/Heaven/Universe and this is the true meaning of being Enlightened and growing in wisdom.

In resume, **Enlightenment is the sum of many little insights. Wisdom is a divine knowledge attained according to the level of consciousness of each one of us.**

For example, Jesus of Nazareth and Siddhārtha Gautama (Budha), they were Enlightened.

I do believe they existed and they were in my eyes great masters, but you don't have to see it in the same way, I respect that; in that case just think about the stories or legends that you probably heard, OK? – I'm mentioning them because what I feel about them is that they are great examples of how enlightenment happens, I think their package of wisdom was higher level than the average of people and they weren't happy about life, how people were living life in such a meaningless way, they wanted more – they were looking for answers and left in search of themselves, they understood that the approach to enlightenment and spiritual growth is not attained through intellectual methods, they needed more profound teachings to satisfy their quest. And like every one of us, they experienced pain, hurt, misunderstanding and judgement: they experienced love and hate, they made mistakes and created contradictions in their lives. It was the completeness of these experiences which made what they became. They were able to transform their own spiritual journey into great knowledge, into great teachings.

Your life, my life is a spiritual journey and we are evolving too, therefore we also can become enlightened just like Jesus, just like Siddhārtha.

Now, no matter if you're enlightened and have a great wisdom, please don't be arrogant, be humble because the same way nature blessed you, nature can also take from you.

Nothing is yours if you don't share it with the right mind.

We can be eternal but we are not here forever. The better you do in this life time, the higher Soul's PhD you get. Isn't that the purpose of life before **Transition**?

# Transition

Heaven or Hell does not exist; neither there is a man with a long beard and white robes who decides if after we die we will go to one side or the other. Heaven is everywhere, as well as Hell; all depends on the level of consciousness of each one of us.

However, I do believe there are spiritual beings that accompany/guide us during our physical life and also in our transition. Some people call them angels, some other like to think that they are the loved ones who already made their transition; you can call them whatever you want if it helps you to understand better, but remember that these are Energy Beings, these beings are not man or woman, these beings don't necessarily have a name, age, race or nationality, these beings are ENERGY.

Sometimes we live life without giving it a great significance. And what happens?

– We do not grow, we do not evolve. In each single human Life, there is a soul and our souls have come into this world, not to suffer but to experience spiritual evolution.

When we evolve, when we grow more and more, we get closer to the Origin:

"Origin of all things."

At the time of transition, we will know what went wrong, if we have to come back to repair what we missed out and how much we could have had been; we will know the frequency (Vibration) achieved during our physical life. The older people use to say and that is no coincidence – "The time of death is the moment of truth", that is because it is when we realise the immensity that we are, the expansive beings that we are, the energy and infinite wisdom that we are.

We limit ourselves so much, either because we just see that we are only a body living in this world and nothing else beyond the physical existence or because we simply cannot see there is an immense Universe in each of us (this limitless feel perhaps like when we face a very strong light, so strong that we can't open our eyes). We are big, we are a beautiful Universe of Energy.

*"Everything is worthwhile if the soul is not small."*

*~ Fernando Pessoa ~*

Live your life with JOY!

# Blessing for Death

*I pray that you will have the blessing of being consoled and sure about your own death.*
*May you know in your soul that there is no need to be afraid?*
*When your time comes, may you be given every blessing and shelter that you need.*
*May there be a beautiful welcome for you in the home that you are going to.*
*You are not going somewhere strange. You are going back to the home that you never left.*
*May you have a wonderful urgency to live your life to the full?*
*May you live compassionately and creatively and transfigure everything that is negative within you and about you.*
*When you come to die may it be after a long life.*
*May you be peaceful and happy and in the presence of those who really care for you.*
*May your going be sheltered and your welcome assured.*
*May your soul smile in the embrace of your Anam Cara.*

*Anam Cara*[5]
*A Book of Celtic Wisdom*
*by John O'Donohue*

---

[5] **Anam Cara** *Anam is the Gaelic word for soul; Cara is the word for friend. So, Anam Cara means soul-friend.*

# Thoughts

*"Thoughts are the expression of inner world, our own invisible world."*

~ *John O'Donohue* ~

## Truth

We all like to win, we all like to be right. We all want our truth to be more truthful.

But **the truth is not about being right, it's doing the right thing!**

Doing the right thing is not always to follow the moral and ethical codes of the society.

Society also need a waking up from time to time.

**It's NOT necessary to go against the rules but we need to think before following the great mass just because it's fashion.** We tend to think to be happy we should engage with the society and it's true, I agree; whether we like it or not we have our duty too. But do we really need to try to be a copy of each other?

Sometimes I feel that we are manipulated, but better not go in that direction, I don't want you to accuse me of conspiracy.

Of course, we cannot simply isolate ourselves into the mountain or in a monastery.

It's OK to do so every now and then; sometimes we need that time of reflection, but not forever. Do you know why? Nature won't bless us. Nature needs us to grow and evolve.

We all have different paths and we all have different steps in life. We all seek the Truth.

If you ask me what my Truth is, I would answer to you the words in this book, but nothing is permanent and what seems so True to me right now may be completely false/wrong tomorrow.

## Information Slavery

In my early 20s I used to say: "The worst enemy of the Humanity is the human intelligence." Perhaps it was my fear of the advancement of technology and the fast development to expose information.

Information is now available everywhere and easily accessible that we almost don't need to attend school. In a certain way, we are so fortunate to be able to simply turn on the computer, connect to internet and *tada*...

However, we need to be aware that most of us are turning into information slaves. We need to be selective and being selective doesn't mean to focus only on what seems to be positive. Being selective means that you recognise if the information/message is for you.

The source of information can come to you from different sources, internet, media, conversations and even situations that you witness.

If some kind of info keeps coming to you, no matter if by hearing, seeing, witnessing, reading, that means there is some message for you to take care of. In case you read something, for example, but didn't have any impact in you that means it's not for you.

And again, in spite of the fact that I may be repeating myself, I would like to remind you of what is true today may not be tomorrow.

## Insights

*"We are not human beings having a spiritual experience.*
*We are spiritual beings having a human experience."*
*~ Pierre Teilhard de Chardin ~*

Seems to me very true, we are all spiritual beings experiencing a human life. It's not that you believe in God or understand all about Ki-Energy phenomena that makes you spiritual.

What makes you to EXPERIENCE your SPIRITUALITY is how much attention you pay to your insights. Through life, we receive many insights and these are not to be neglected but respected as these could be a help to governing your life independently of the religion or philosophy you follow. We all have different paths and we're all in this world to grow the spiritual being inside us, no matter the way you choose to do it. And insights are just there almost everywhere in our everyday life, sometimes very subtle and difficult to recognise.

An insight could be almost a eureka moment where things suddenly start to make more sense.

I believe that we have chosen the package that we came in and that's why we are all spiritual beings, although you may not recognise yourself as spiritual.

Insights are to be used so you can understand more about Elemental Energy, native to each one of us – True Self / Higher Self.

Insights are to be realised so you can understand life and prevent mistakes. These small personal mistakes and the unawareness of its repetition are the reason for so much unhappiness and illnesses.

> *"Illness is equal to the accumulation of many small mistakes."*
>
> ~ *Master Jinjung* ~

If you realise the so-called mistakes/contradictions of your life, your energy will change and it is this change that you can understand as miracles.

### Miracles = Conscious Energy
(Please note the package that I'm talking about is the 30% mentioned in the chapter 'Victim Behaviour and Destiny'.)

# Self-Awareness

*"Let go of your story so the Universe can write a new one for you."*

*~ Marianne Williamson ~*

We all want our life to be better. We all compare our life to others (at least once); we just see what we want to see, not what reality really is. As someone said: "The grass is always greener on the other side."

We all want some sort of change to happen, but the reality is that we often do very little for that change to happen. Is so much easier to hold onto what's already known… the drama of our own life…

Many of you become really busy in talking about the issues of your lives as if you have some kind of hidden pleasure by keeping on speaking like a tape recorder; it's the past that you may carry on your shoulders or the present that's bothering or the lack of hope for the future… I understand, it's a way of getting attention and some affection from others, which perhaps you do it unconsciously or it's already a habit: I understand that you got stuck into these feelings but you aren't giving a chance to yourself to see the possibilities/opportunities presented to you. No matter how much you try to be positive or practicing the law of attraction, if you don't work on trying to detach from whatever is disturbing you. The problem here is that people around you may feel tired and even sick of you; they may love you very much and they try their best to help you, but if you don't help yourself, there isn't much that they can do for you and at certain stage it's hard to be with someone who's sorry for him/herself most of the time.

I'm not talking about depression, that's a different case, that's a more complex subject and requires a completely different perspective. Depressed people are someone with huge energy, not knowing how big is that and how to utilise it for higher purpose and normally these people are not sorry for themselves, they just have no hope in the future, in the world.

*"We all have different types of intelligence, various types of
memory and many egos. And it is time for us to awaken to
the more valuable although basic aspects of consciousness
and let go of mediatic usage of 'Here and Now'."*
~ *Waldo Vieira* ~

Self-awareness is the attempt to change what we don't like
about ourselves (without begging for attention, though), bring
our talents out of the closet (even if it feels 'unpolished') and
realising the blessings in and of our lives.

## Alien Syndrome
No, I'm not going to talk about aliens, but about the feeling
that some of us have as if not belonging to this world, as if not
fitting somehow in this life...
    – Do you feel alien in this world?
    This is the kind of subject that can be delicate and
deceptive. Yet I dare to say that the motive that causes us to
feel this way is related to the fact that our spirit may have been
in that other dimension, that non-physical world more than
200, 500, 1000 years (I don't believe that a person after dying
could come back in a very short period of time, although the
concept of time doesn't exist in the world of spirit); therefore,
I think that it would be normal for us to miss the sense of
unity, oneness that defines the world of spirit. As you know,
Soul is no matter, uses our body to sort out the karma and to
rise in consciousness. The Soul knows somehow what to do
and that's why we come back to the physical world, the
challenge is quieting our mind in order to access to our
Higher/True Self and acknowledge the Great Wisdom.

*"The Soul always knows what to do to heal itself. The
challenge is to silence the mind."*
~ *Rumi* ~

# The Great Wisdom

The Great Wisdom, what's that?

I wish I could say exactly what that is, but I can't. I believe or I just want to believe there is something else greater than the physical life.

Seems to me that Life itself is not enough. It feels meaningless just being born, growing up, getting a job, perhaps getting married and becoming parents, work endlessly to have some comfort and give a good education to the children or providing care to the old parents, travel around a few countries to feel a bit more alive and that's it really... Is this a blissful life?

There has to be something more; something magical; something that most of us are looking forward to find out; the hidden secret of Consciousness and Spirit; the treasure.

The treasure is composed not only with the teachings which life provides us with, but also the magical answers to the deeper existential questions. I suppose that our Soul (we all have different levels and that's why we may have many lives) is acquiring a degree in consciousness in each Step of Life until the secret is completely revealed and we're ready to understand what Great Wisdom could be. The Great Wisdom is a journey, the Secret – a PhD.

# Blessings

Talking about blessings can be quite tricky, because what could be felt as blessing by me might not be by you. A bit of rain may be seen as a blessing in Saudi Arabia but a warmer weather time to time would be more welcomed in Scotland; which means the way we perceive blessing is different; perhaps for you a smile from someone in the street is a blessing and for someone else it doesn't mean anything, isn't that right? Although we all have a different way of perceiving, we all can feel there is something in life so precious that money cannot bring. In matter of a fact, if you pay attention to people's comments what they mention as important in life are the little, the simple things; for example – I was brought up in the country side, where people used to have little green garden and a few fruit trees (I know I was young, but probably back then I just took it as granted) – now, when I'm back home and being able to pick up the fruit directly from the tree or go to the garden and collect some fresh vegetables, is for me a real blessing. Another example, one of these days I went to the grocery shopping and when I went back to my car, I had a very interesting message on the windshield saying:

"Hi, you are a sexy chick whom I fancy. Shay." – This was for me another blessing.

(Shay, if you are reading this by now, I want you to know that I really appreciated it).

Blessings are what you give **value**.

We need to learn to see the good in us and around us, the little things.

Blessings are **awakenings.**

Not always blessings start from being something that we consider good; e.g. – you're going on a trip and you took the wrong road but end up in the most beautiful place.

Blessings are **reminders**.

We are so busy fulfilling our lives with meaningless stuff that we often forget there are the little details that can make the difference, like the little note on my windshield which reminded me to care more for my female energy.

May you be blessed with good health, love and joy.

# Butterfly

The butterfly flies.
It simply flies. Comes to rest, stays for a while and then flies off.
Without attaching itself to anything or anyone. Its only concern is in making the forest more beautiful.
It carries everything and everyone in its butterfly heart, and nothing more.
It does not depend on them.
It does not depend on their love or their presence.
It only loves. It loves and flies. It loves and flies.
Be like a butterfly.
Do not become attached to anything or anyone.
Keep everything inside your heart.
Love and fly. And make the forest a more beautiful place.

                                                                            Jesus

                                    Message 208; "The Book of Light"
                                             by Alexandra Solnado

# References

~ *Rumi* ~
(September 30, 1207 – December 17, 1273)
Persian Sunni; Muslim poet, jurist, Islamic scholar, theologian and Sufi mystic.

~ *Alan Watts* ~
(January 6, 1915 – November 16, 1973)
British philosopher, writer, and speaker, best known as an interpreter and populariser of Eastern philosophy for a Western audience.

~ *Lao Tzu* ~
(6th century)
Ancient Chinese philosopher and writer. He is known as the reputed author of the *Tao Te Ching* and the founder of philosophical Taoism, and as a deity in religious Taoism and traditional Chinese religions.

~ *Master Jinjung* ~
South Korean Master
http://www.thegreatestlaw.org/
https://www.facebook.com/jungbub.boston/
Some of his work is translated into English in YouTube – "Jinjung's Dharma Talk"

~ *Kahlil Gibran* ~
(January 6, 1883 – April 10, 1931)
Lebanese-American artist, poet, and writer of the New York Pen League.

~ *Fernando Pessoa* ~
(June 13, 1888 – November 30, 1935)
Portuguese poet, writer, literary critic, translator, publisher and philosopher, described as one of the most significant

literary figures of the 20th century and one of the greatest poets in the Portuguese language.

~ *Alexandra Solnado* ~

(November 11, 1964)

Alexandra Solnado is an international spiritual healer, a beloved spiritual teacher and one of Portugal's bestselling authors. Currently, she is the director of the project Therapy for the Soul, which includes several therapists, giving courses on personal spiritual development and a series of spiritual therapies.

http://www.alexandrasolnado.net

~ *Soledad O'Brien* ~

(Born September 19, 1966)

American broadcast journalist and executive producer. Currently, O'Brien is the anchor for *Matter of Fact with Soledad O'Brien,* a weekly show on Hearst Television. She is chairwoman of Starfish Media Group, a multi-platform media production company and distributor that she founded in 2013.

~ *Nelson Mandela* ~

(July 18, 1918 – December 5, 2013)

South African anti-apartheid revolutionary, politician, and philanthropist, who served as President of South Africa from 1994 to 1999. He was the country's first black head of state and the first elected in a fully representative democratic election. His government focused on dismantling the legacy of apartheid by tackling institutionalised racism and fostering racial reconciliation.

~ *Albert Einstein* ~

(14 March 1879 – 18 April 1955)

German-born theoretical physicist. He developed the general theory of relativity, one of the two pillars of modern physics (alongside quantum mechanics). Einstein's work is also known for its influence on the philosophy of science. Einstein is best known in popular culture for his mass–energy equivalence formula $E = mc^2$ (which has been dubbed "the world's most famous equation")

~ *St, Jerome* ~

(Born in 347 – September 30, 420)

Born at Stridon, north eastern Italy. Priest, confessor, theologian and historian. He is best known for his translation of most of the Bible into Latin and his commentaries on the Gospels.

~ *Mother Teresa* ~

(August 26, 1910 – September 5, 1997)

Mother Teresa known in the Catholic Church as Saint Teresa of Calcutta. In 1950 Teresa founded the Missionaries of Charity, a Roman Catholic religious congregation which had over 4,500 sisters and was active in 133 countries in 2012. The congregation manages homes for people dying of HIV/AIDS, leprosy and tuberculosis; soup kitchens; dispensaries and mobile clinics; children's- and family-counselling programmes; orphanages, and schools. Members, who take vows of chastity, poverty, and obedience, also profess a fourth vow: to give "wholehearted free service to the poorest of the poor".

~ **Pierre Teilhard de Chardin** ~

(May 1, 1881 – April 10, 1955)

French idealist philosopher and Jesuit priest who trained as palaeontologist and geologist and took part in the discovery of Peking Man. He conceived the vitalism idea of the Omega Point (a maximum level of complexity and consciousness towards which he believed the universe was evolving) and developed Vladimir Vernadsky's concept of noosphere.

~ **John O'Donohue** ~

(January 1, 1956 – January 4, 2008)

Was an Irish poet, author, priest, and Hegelian philosopher. He was a native Irish speaker, and as an author is best known for popularising Celtic spirituality. And these are some of his work: Anam Cara; Eternal Echoes; Divine Beauty; Echoes of Memory.

~ **Waldo Vieira** ~

(April 12, 1932 – July 2, 2015)

Brazilian physician and medium who first proposed the theories of projectiology and conscientiology, two closely related nascent sciences which posit that human consciousness is a non-physical phenomenon. He has written various books on vital energy, parapsychical and personal development, and out-of-body experiences. He has been among the most prolific authors on the subject.

## ~ Marianne Williamson ~

(July 8, 1952)

American spiritual teacher, author and lecturer who has published eleven books. Founder of Project Angel Food, a meals-on-wheels program that serves homebound people with AIDS in the Los Angeles area, and the co-founder of The Peace Alliance, a grassroots campaign supporting legislation to establish a United States Department of Peace. She serves on the Board of Directors of the RESULTS organisation, which works to end poverty in the United States and around the world. Williamson also produces the Sister Giant Conferences, highlighting the intersection of spirituality and politics.

## ~ Mahatma Gandhi ~

(October 2, 1869 – January 30, 1948)

Leader of the Indian independen ce movement against British rule. Employing nonviolent civil disobedience, Gandhi led India to independence and inspired movements for civil rights and freedom across the world. Gandhi's birthday, 2 October, is commemorated in India as Gandhi Jayanti, a national holiday, and worldwide as the International Day of Nonviolence.

*\* Please note that most of these references are based on the collected information from Wikipedia \**